Like the people living there, New York City is generous, diverse and full of surprises. A nexus of opportunities and dreams, a financial centre, political stage and international platform for entertainment and performance art. Mavericks flock here to test ideas, and young artists come to get their voices heard. Everyone wants to be a part of this city. A city where every desire can be satisfied.

CITIx60: New York explores the Big Apple in five aspects, covering architecture, art spaces, shops and markets, eating and entertainments. With expert advice from 60 stars of New York City's creative scene, this book guides you to the real attractions of the city for an authentic taste of New York life.

Contents

P9-CSU-705

WITHDRAWN

Before You Go

BASIC INFO

Currency
U.S. Dollar (USD/$)
Exchange rate: $1 : €0.8

Time zone
GMT −5
DST −4

DST begins at 0200 (local time) on the second Sunday in March and ends at 0200 (local time) on the first Sunday in November.

Dialling
International calling: +1
Citywide: 212, 917, 718, 646, 347, 929, 332

*Always include area code for calls. Dial 1 for domestic calls, or 001 for calls made outside the US.

Weather (avg. temperature range)
Spring (Late Mar–May): 3–20°C / 37–68°F
Summer (Jun–Aug): 20–30°C / 68–86°F
Autumn (Sep–Nov): 5–20°C / 41–68°F
Winter (Dec–Mar): −5–8°C / 23–47°F

USEFUL WEBSITES

MTA Bus & Subway
mta.info

Visa application
travel.state.gov/content/travel/en/us-visas.html

EMERGENCY CALLS

Ambulance, fire or police
911

Multilingual visitor information counsellors
+1 (212) 48 41 222

Consulates
China   +1 (212) 86 82 078
Japan   +1 (212) 37 18 222
France   +1 (212) 60 63 600
Germany +1 (212) 61 09 700
UK   +1 (212) 74 50 200

AIRPORT EXPRESS TRANSFERS

JFK Airport <−> Manhattan (AirTrain JFK)
Trains / Journey: every 5–20 mins / 35 mins
From airport or Manhattan (Penn Station)
(Change for Long Island Rail Road @Jamaica Station) – 24hrs, $15 (one-way)

LaGuardia Airport <−> Manhattan (NYC Airporter)
Buses / Journey: every 30 mins / 60 mins
From airport or Manhattan (Penn Station) –
0600–2330, $16 (one-way)

EWR Airport <−> Manhattan (AirTrain Newark)
Trains / Journey: every 3–15 mins / 30 mins
From airport – 24hrs
From Manhattan (Penn Station) (Change for NJ TRANSIT @Newark Liberty Airport Station) – 0500–0200, $12.50 (one-way)

www.panynj.gov/airports

PUBLIC TRANSPORT IN NYC

MTA Bus & Subway*
Railroad
Citi Bike
Taxi
Uber/Lyft

*Free subway–bus or bus–subway transfers within 2 hours of using your MetroCard.

FEDERAL / BANK HOLIDAYS

January	1 New Year's Day*, Martin Luther King Jr. Day (3rd Mon)
February	12 Lincoln's Birthday, Washington's Birthday (3rd Mon)
May	Memorial Day (Last Mon)
July	4 Independence Day
September	Labour Day (1st Mon)
October	Columbus Day (2nd Mon)
November	General Election Day (Tue after 1st Mon), 11 Veterans Day, Thanksgiving Day (4th Thu)*
December	25 Christmas Day*

If a bank holiday falls on a weekend, the next weekday becomes a 'substitute' day. Cultural institutions and shops might be closed on *days.

FESTIVALS / EVENTS

January
Première Vision Fashion Fair (also in July)
www.premierevision-newyork.com

February
New York Fashion Week (also in September)
www.mbfashionweek.com

March
The Armory Show
thearmoryshow.com

April
The AIGA Awards Gala
www.aiga.org/AIGA-awards

May
NYCxDESIGN
nycxdesign.com
International Contemporary Furniture Fair
www.icff.com
WantedDesign
www.wanteddesignnyc.com

June
NYC Pride
www.nycpride.org

September
NY Art Book Fair by Printed Matter
nyartbookfair.com

October
Open House New York Weekend
ohny.org

November
NYC Marathon
www.ingnycmarathon.org
Macy's Thanksgiving Day Parade
social.macys.com/parade

December
Times Square New Year's Eve
timessquarenyc.org

Event days vary by year. Please check for
updates online.

UNUSUAL OUTINGS

Broadway Up Close
www.broadwayupclose.com

Big Onion Walking Tours
www.bigonion.com

Get Up And Ride
www.getupandride.com

Musuem Hack
www.museumhack.com

Municipal Art Society of New York Tours
mas.org/tours

Navy Yard Seasonal Photography Tours
bldg92.org/visit/public-tours

SMARTPHONE APPS

Event & entertainment listings
The Scoop (iOS only)

Bike routes, locator & available bikes / docks
CityVelo NY (iOS only)

Live bus times & route maps
NYC Bus Checker

REGULAR EXPENSES

Cappuccino
$3.50-$5

**Domestic / International mail (standard post-
cards)**
$0.35 / $1.15

Gratuities
Restaurants & bars: 15-25% of total bill,
$1-2 per drink
Hotels: $2-5/hailed cab for doormen, $1-2/bag for
porters or bellhops, $2-5/night for cleaners,
$5/dinner or ticket reservation for concierge
Licensed taxis: 15-20%
Services: $1-2 for valet parking, coat checks or
bathroom attendants; 15-25% for hairdressers,
manicurists, masseuses or tour guides

Count to 10

What makes New York City so special?

Illustrations by Guillaume Kashima aka Funny Fun

To many out-of-towners, New York City is an intense city with much to absorb. To locals, it's a home filled with the sound of car horns, trains on tracks, sirens and people yelling in the streets, every part of it special in its own way. Whether you are on a one-day stopover or a week-long stay, see what New York creatives consider essential to see, taste, read and take home from your trip.

1

Museums & Galleries

MoMA
www.moma.org

The Guggenheim (#17)
www.guggenheim.org

The Metropolitan Museum of Art
www.metmuseum.org

Museum of Art and Design
madmuseum.org

Whitney Museum of American Art
whitney.org

Dia:Beacon, The Earth Room & The Broken Kilometer
www.diaart.org

Brooklyn Museum
www.brooklynmuseum.org

Neue Galerie
www.neuegalerie.org

CUT, SHAVE & TRIM @The barber shop

5

Fashion

Cut, shave, trim
The Blind Barber
blindbarber.com

Quality apparel
Only NY Store
onlyny.com

Sneakers
Alumni Shoes
alumniofny.com

Tattoo
NY Adorned
www.nyadorned.com

Fine jewellery
Jennifer Fisher Jewelry
jenniferfisherjewelry.com

6

Live Gigs & Performances

The Mercury Lounge
www.mercuryloungenyc.com

Music Hall of Williamsburg
www.musichallofwilliamsburg.com

Terminal 5
www.terminal5nyc.com

Radio City Music Hall
www.radiocity.com

Joe's Pub
www.joespub.com

Broadway theatres
www.broadway.com

American Ballet Theatre
www.abt.org

7

Art Books & International Reads

Printed Matter
printedmatter.org

Bookmarc by Marc Jacobs
www.marcjacobs.com/bookmarc

192 BOOKS
www.192books.com

McNally Jackson
mcnallyjackson.com

The POWERHOUSE Arena (#31)
www.powerhousearena.com

WORD
wordbookstores.com

Spoonbill & Sugartown
www.spoonbillbooks.com

8

Leisure

Jog
Central Park (#1)

Ice skating
The Rink at Rockefeller Center (#10)
therinkatrockcenter.com

Watch a baseball game
mlb.com

**Share your story
or listen to one**
The Moth
themoth.org

**Stare at the commuters
& be stared at**
On any subway line

Ride the wonder wheel
www.denoswonderwheel.com

Get a thermal bath
AIRE ancient baths
www.ancientbathsny.com

9

Cultural Legends

Keith Haring
www.haring.com

Andy Warhol
The Factory (3rd location)
860 Broadway,
Flatiron District, 10003

Woody Allen
The Duplex
(Venue of Allen's debut stand-up)
www.theduplex.com

Louis Armstrong
Louis Armstrong House Museum
www.louisarmstronghouse.org

Duke Ellington
Duke Ellington Circle,
Central Park (#1)
www.dukeellington.com

10

Mementos

Authentic NYC garbage
Garbage NYC
nycgarbage.com

Handcrafted chocolate bars
MAST Brooklyn
mastbrothers.com

Hudson Baby Bourbon Whiskey
Tuthilltown
www.tuthilltown.com

**Gold Empire State Building
necklace**
Canal St., SoHo, 10013

**A "Return to Tiffany"
heart tag key chain**
Tiffany & Co. Flagship
727 5th Av., Midtown East, 10022

"I ♥ NY" tourist tee & kitsch
Memories of New York
www.memoriesofnewyork.com

Icon Index

 Opening hours

 Address

 Contact

Remarks

 Admission

 Facebook

 Website

 Scan QR codes to access Google Maps and discover the area around each destination. Internet connection required.

60x60

60 Local Creatives x 60 Hotspots

From vast cityscapes to the smallest snippets of conversation, there is much to inspire creative urges in New York City. 60x60 points you to 60 haunts where 60 arbiters of taste develop their nose for the good stuff.

Landmarks & Architecture
SPOTS · 01 – 12

Discover the city's palpable pride and personality through its world famous skyline and cultural landmarks, visitable by foot, bike, boat or any number of other ways.

Cultural & Art Spaces
SPOTS · 13 – 24

Consider NYC one huge art gallery. Besides classic bricks and mortar museums and galleries, an endless flow of public work throbs across the city, just waiting to be found.

Markets & Shops
SPOTS · 25 – 36

Complete your ultimate lifestyle checklist with iconic New York labels, recognisable groceries, books, vinyls, art prints and delicacies. Prepare cash and shop till you drop.

Restaurants & Cafés
SPOTS · 37 – 48

Work up your appetite. Kitchens for every taste deliver bona fide New York classics from bagels to pizza and hot dogs alongside the World's Fair of ethnic cuisine.

Nightlife
SPOTS · 49 – 60

Sleep only when you leave NYC because wild parties are awaiting. If you want peace and quiet, the city's waterfront parks and selective art spaces are your place.

Landmarks & Architecture

Iconic buildings, popular parks & Manhattan skyline's best spots

Once skyscrapers start to shadow and the streets get progressively more packed, you know you're getting to the heart of New York City. Of the five boroughs – The Bronx, Brooklyn, Manhattan, Queens and Staten Island – Manhattan is the smallest, yet most heavily populated, and is home to the world's largest stock market, multinational companies and newsrooms. The city's distinctive gridded streets were introduced in the 1811 grid plan. Where Central Park (#1) has long been inseparable from New Yorkers' lives, new parks like The High Line (#4) and Brooklyn Bridge Park (#2) are also grabbing locals' (and big-name architects') hearts. Want to explore a world outside the island? Take the A train (or F train) or walk across the Brooklyn Bridge to Dumbo and Brooklyn. Bedford Avenue, for example, has a unique cultural anthropology–through–architecture offering. Starting from Russian-concentrated Brighton Beach at the southern end, you will encounter the old-money Jewish suburbs, ivy-bedecked Brooklyn College, Little Israel and Polish Greenpoint as you travel north. Alternatively, try a helicopter ride or take a free round trip on the Staten Island Ferry for a view of Lower Manhattan. The New York Harbour is one of the deepest natural harbours in the world.

Frederick Bouchardy
Fragrance designer, JOYA

A native New Yorker born at University Hospital near Union Square. Bouchardy has a gold-en-eyed puppy named Clay.

Brooklyn Bridge Park 015

Jennifer Fisher
Jewellery designer

Native Californian and now a NY transplant. Fisher lives with her family in Tribeca and is constantly trying new things in the city. The recommended are our favourites.

Keegan McHargue
Artist

American painter and sculptor born in 1982 at Portland, Oregon, currently living and working in New York.

Central Park 014

FDR Four Freedoms Park 016

jeffstaple
Creative director, Staple Design

Founder and Creative Director of Staple Design and Reed Space.

Tribeca Synagogue 018

Shohei Shigematsu
Architect

Partner of OMA New York since 2008. Under his direction, OMA has overseen the completion of Cornell University Milstein Hall and the building of National Beaux Arts museum, Quebec.

Jessica Walsh
Partner, Sagmeister & Walsh

Designer and art director, named "Young Gun" by Art Director's Club. Walsh also teaches at the School of Visual Arts (NYC) and speaks interna-tionally about her work.

The High Line 017

New Museum 019

Lotta Nieminen
Art director & graphic designer

Originally from Helsinki. Nieminen's clients include Hermès, New York Times, Volkswagen, United Airlines, Monocle, Newsweek, Wired UK and Bloomberg Businessweek.

Jane's
Carousel
020

41 Cooper
Square
021

Lucie Kim
Founder, MyORB

Founder and creative director of MyORB, which creates identities, websites, typefaces, books, design exhibitions, short films, and make other things that are playful, curious and intriguing.

Nathan Sawaya
Artist

A trained attorney who creates large-scale sculptures using only LEGO bricks, author of two best-sellers, and owner of more than 2.5 million coloured bricks in his art studios in NY and LA.

New York
Public Library
Main Branch
024

Matthew Waldman
Founder, Nooka Inc.

Best known for my brand Nooka, I am a designer and artist whose work brings the optimism of futurism to lifestyle. My magic party trick is speaking fluent Japanese.

Rockefeller
Center
025

Seagram
Building
026

Jing Liu
Architect & co-founder, SO-IL

New Yorker, architect, mother of two, Brooklynite, world traveller, trilingual, dancer, food-lover, 30 something, founding partner of SO-IL, Chinese, Southern accent.

Riitta Ikonen
Photographer

Originally from the deep eastern forests of Finland, but is now a fresh New Yorker and keen collaborator working mainly with photographers and costume.

James A.
Farley Post
Office
027

1 Central Park
Map J, P.110

Popularly referred to as the lungs of the New York City, Central Park is an 843-acre architectural masterpiece designed by Frederick Law Olmsted and Calvert Vaux in the 1850s. It was designated the city's first scenic landmark in 1974 and is believed to be the most filmed location in the world. Integral to New Yorkers' life, the park notably contains natural-looking lakes, woodlands, a reservoir, bridle paths, and two ice skating rinks – one of which converts to an outdoor swimming pool in summer. Neighbouring features include the MET, and the American Museum of Natural History to its east and west.

🕒 0600–0100 daily
🏠 Central Park, 10028
📞 +1 (212) 310 6600
🌐 www.centralparknyc.org

"Just walk and breathe in the linden blossoms. Or take a guided tour through Central Park Conservancy and check out the Conservatory Garden."

– Frederick Bouchardy

2 Brooklyn Bridge Park
Map C, P.106

Stretching 1.3 miles along Brooklyn's East River edge, Brooklyn Bridge Park is a repurposed post-industrial site for a multiplicity of recreational areas and public programmes set against the spectacular view of Brooklyn bridge, harbour and lower Manhattan. Although the transformation is still in progress, the park exhibits remarkable sustainable designs and measures planned by landscape architects Michael Van Valkenburgh Associates. Future park sections will include Brooklyn Bridge Plaza and additional piers, alongside fishing points and a calm water boating zone. Check out nearby Modern Anthology on Jay street for some good vintage and designer finds.

🕐 0600-0100 daily
🏠 334 Furman St.,
Brooklyn Heights, 11201
📞 +1 (718) 222 9939
URL www.brooklynbridgepark.org

"It is the greatest piece of architecture in New York in my mind. Walk it on a nice day, grab pizza at Grimaldis then water taxi it back."
– Jennifer Fisher, Jennifer Fisher Jewelry

3 **FDR Four Freedoms Park**
Map A, P.103 / Map K, P.110

Proposed in 1973 but not realised until October 2012, FDR Four Freedoms Park celebrates the life and work of the late US president Franklin D. Roosevelt with special tributes to the Four Freedoms – freedom of speech, freedom of worship, freedom from want and freedom from fear – articulated in his 1941 State of the Union address. Architect Louis Kahn was tasked with the planning, although he died shortly after finishing his design. The island was named Roosevelt Island in the president's honour the same year the project was announced.

◷ 0900–1700 (W–M)
🏠 1 FDR Four Freedoms Park, Roosevelt Island, 10044
☎ +1 (212) 204 8831
URL www.fdrfourfreedomspark.org

"The design itself is from a past era, but it feels contemporary in its formal and symmetrical concerns."
– Keegan McHargue

4 The High Line
Map A, P.102

Originally built for freight trains in the 1930s, The High Line is now reopened as an elevated promenade and public park surrounded by notable architecture. View Jean Nouvel's window-clad condominium and Shigeru Ban's Metal Shutter House next to a Frank Gehry office building, and the Renzo Piano-designed Whitney Museum of American Art on the south end of the park. Created by James Corner Field Operations, Diller Scofidio + Renfro and Piet Oudolf, the park features meandering pathways, local vegetation and free recreational programmes for everyone to enjoy.

🕐 0700-2200 daily, -2300 (Jun-Sep), -1900 (Dec-Mar)
🏠 Gansevoort St. to W. 34th St., Manhattan, 10011
📞 +1 (212) 500 6035 **URL** www.thehighline.org
✏️ Park may be partially closed due to bad weather

"Sun sets in the West, so go at sunset for some amazing views!"
– jeffstaple, Staple Design

5 Tribeca Synagogue
Map B, P.104

Synagogue for the Arts is a full-service Jewish house of prayer and art gallery in Tribeca, the industrial-turned-upscale area in Lower Manhattan. Originally founded as the Civic Center Synagogue in 1938, the building was designed by William Breger, a student of Bauhaus bigwig Walter Gropius (1883-1969). Completed in 1967, a massive, curvy façade over a glass-walled entrance is consciously set back to align with the properties in and around White street. The main sanctuary is a bright, sky-lit area behind the façade, where local communities go to daven and meditate.

🕐 *By appointment only*
🏠 *49 White St., Tribeca, 10013*
📞 *+1 (212) 966 7141*
URL *www.tribecasynagogue.org*

6 New Museum
Map B, P.105

Architects of New Museum building Kazuyo Sejima and Ryue Nishizawa of SANAA have described the work as their response to the powerful personalities of both the New Museum and the surrounding storied neighbourhood. They were challenged to devise open, flexible and light-filled gallery spaces of different atmospheres and heights within a very tight zoning. Viewed as a dramatic stack of seven rectangular boxes, rising 175 feet above street level amidst a cluster of small and mid-sized buildings on the Bowery, the New Museum building itself perhaps best describes the new ideas of contemporary art it collects.

🕙 1100–1800 (Tu–W, F–Su), –2100 (Th)
💲 $18/15/12/Pay-as-you-wish (Th: 1900–2100)
🏠 235 Bowery, Manhattan, 10002
📞 +1 (212) 219 1222 URL www.newmuseum.org
🖉 Free docent tours: 1230 (Tu–Su), 1500 (Th, Sa, Su)

"Interesting building located right in the heart of Soho. Check out their shows as well as the shopping and restaurants in the area."
– Jessica Walsh, Sagmeister & Walsh

7 Jane's Carousel
Map C, P.107

After decades of meticulous restoration by Jane Walentas this nearly century-old Carousel now beams brightly on the edge of the East River. Framed by the Williamsburg Bridge to the north, Brooklyn Bridge to the south, and encased inside a glass jewel-box pavilion designed by Pritzker winning architect Jean Nouvel, Manhattan's skyline is its backdrop. The three-row machine features 48 exquisitely carved horses and two superb chariots, originally installed in Idora Park in Youngstown, Ohio.

🕐 Mid-May to mid-Sep: 1100–1900 (W–M);
Mid-Sep to mid-May: –1800 (Th–Su) 💲 $2
🏠 Old Dock St., Dumbo, Brooklyn, 11201
📞 +1 (718) 222 2502
URL www.janescarousel.com

"The view from Brooklyn Bridge Park is amazing, but admiring it while riding on a carousel is even better."
– Lotta Nieminen

41 Cooper Square is the first LEED-certified academic laboratory building in NYC. Designed by Pritzker-winning Thom Mayne of Morphosis Architects, the centre's distinctive appearance and technological innovation alluded to The Cooper Union's dedication to free, open and accessible education in art, architecture and engineering, and fosters cross-disciplinary dialogue within. Green building initiatives include a full-height atrium to increase interior daylight and a cogeneration plant to provide additional power and recover waste heat.

🕐 0730–0200 (M–Th), –0000 (F, Sa), 1200–0200 (Su)
🏠 3rd Ave. (b/w 6th & 7th St.), East Village, 10003
📞 +1 (212) 353 4100
🔗 cooper.edu

"Finished in 2009, the building is one of the few recent New York architecture additions that actually work. The long staircase invites students to hang out."

– Lucie Kim

9 New York Public Library Main Branch

Map A, P.103

Officially named "Stephen A. Schwarzman Building," this Beaux-Arts library opened in 1911 houses remarkable research collections in the humanities. The Carrère-and-Hastings building is also noted for its majestic Rose Main Reading Room built on top of seven floors of bookstacks. Norman Foster's plan to replace the stacks in 2013 was vastly criticised for affecting the structure, and led to withdrawal. The marble lions' name "Patience" and "Fortitude" were given by Mayor Fiorello LaGuardia during the 1930s, to symbolise the qualities he felt would be needed to survive the economic woe during the 1930s.

🕐 1000–1800 (M, Th–Sa), –2000 (Tu–W), 1300–1700 (Su)
🏠 476 5th Ave. (at 42nd St.), Murray Hill, 10018
📞 +1 (917) 275 6975 URL www.nypl.org
✐ Free docent tours: 1100 & 1400 (M–Sa)

"*You may know the lions from Ghostbusters. But I also built replicas out of LEGO for the library's 100th birthday. Find them inside the lobby!*"

– Nathan Sawaya

10 Rockefeller Center
Map A, P.103

Beginning as philanthropic venture, John D. Rockefeller, Jr.'s initiative to build a cultural centre in Midtown Manhattan has become today's Rockefeller Center. The complex comprises 14 Art Deco office buildings from the 1930s and four International-style towers built during the 1960s and 1970s. "Art" remains at the nexus of the development with forms of architectural sculpture, including *News* (1904) by Isamu Noguchi (1904–88) and *Atlas* (1937) by Lee Lawrie (1877–1963). The development's centrepiece, the GE Building at 30 Rockefeller Plaza, houses broadcasters NBC's headquarters, with an observation deck offering views of the Big Apple 259 metres above ground level.

 45 Rockefeller Plaza, Manhattan, 10111 🕐 +1 (212) 332 6868
🔗 www.rockefellercenter.com
📎 Top of the Rock: 0800–0000 daily, www.topoftherocknyc.com, $34/32/28

"Get a beautiful view of Manhattan and the Empire State Building from 'Top of the Rock'! In winter, the skating rink is a very iconic NYC tourist thing to do."
– Matthew Waldman, Nooka Inc.

11 **Seagram Building**
Map A, P.103

Wrapped in a curtain wall of bronze mullions and tinted glass windows, the 38-storey skyscraper typifies architect Ludwig Mies van der Rohe's (1886–1969) dictum "Less is more." Symbolic of Seagram Liquor Company's growing power, Mies' first attempt at high-rise office tower construction, built in 1958, presents original concepts, like the inclusion of a forecourt to enhance the building's presence in the urban jungle. Mies' student Philip Johnson (1903–2005) went on to master its lobby and the landmarked Four Seasons, now relocated. Although much of the restaurant's contents has been auctioned, its iconic bar and Richard Lippold sculpture remain at its current occupant, The Grill.

🏠 375 Park Ave., Midtown East, 10152
URL 375parkavenue.com

"Take a walk along Park Avenue from the MetLife building to Seagram, one will understand New York in its most dandy moment."

– Jing Liu, SO-IL

12 James A. Farley Post Office
Map A, P.102

Once the main mail sorting hall for US Postal Service's operations, the building was intended to be a continuation of the now-razed Pennsylvania Station on the Eighth Avenue, both drawn up by architects McKim, Mead and White. Dedicated to the State's 53rd Postmaster in 1982, the 1912 granite structure was famous for its ornate and inscription on the façade, a translated quotation from Herodotus' Histories. The historical building remains open until it is fully converted into Daniel Patrick Moynihan Station, the new intercity train hall for Amtrak.

🕐 0700-2200 (M-F), 0900-2100 (Sa), 1100-1900 (Su)
🏠 421 8th Ave., Chelsea, 10001
📞 +1 (212) 330 3296
🔗 www.uspspostoffices.com/ny/new-york/james-a-farley

"The Farley Post Office is home to 'Operation Santa,' made famous in the classic 1947 film, Miracle on 34th Street."

– Riitta Ikonen

Cultural & Art Spaces

Museums, art galleries and sculpture parks

See as many galleries and museums as you can, but take note, art pieces don't just reside indoors in New York. With the law Percent for Art requiring eligible city-funded building projects to allocate one percent of their budget for public art work, and organisations such as the great Public Art Fund, art lovers should go on a hunt for the results – outdoor sculptures and site-specific projects in all five boroughs. Besides Robert Indiana's iconic LOVE sculpture *(1359 Ave. of the Americas, Midtown East, 10019)*, take a picnic under Piccaso's imposing Bust of Sylvette at I. M. Pei's Silver Towers *(Greenwich Village, 10012)*, visit Socrates Sculpture Park *(32-01 Vernon Blvd., Long Island City, 11106)* or spend a night or two outside town visiting Storm King Art Center (#13) and Dia:Beacon *(3 Beekman St., Beacon, 12508)*. For more surreal experiences, late master Walter de Maria's (1935–2013) permanent installations "The Earth Room" *(141 Wooster St., SoHo, 10012)* and "The Broken Kilometer" *(393 W. Broadway, SoHo, 10012)* are worth a trip. Brooklyn Navy Yard Center at BLDG 92 *(63 Flushing Ave., Brooklyn, 11205)* should also be on every urban explorer's list. Check out the museum's exhibitions, and join one of the amazing tours, including the fantastic seasonal photo tour. Avoid Sundays for most galleries, and weekends for classics like The Guggenheim (#17), the Met, MoMA and American Museum of Natural History around the Central Park.

Chelsea Art District, P.040

Sean Dougherty
Director, Brand New School

Creative director and director at Brand New School NYC office. I live in Brooklyn and am enjoying the current food renaissance happening here.

MoMA PS1
033

Laurent Barthelemy
Animator & designer

Born in a small town in the south of France, but now lives in New York City with his wife Shizuka and four-year-old daughter June.

Craig Redman
Graphic designer, Craig & Karl

Creator of Darcel Disappoints and one half of Craig & Karl.

Storm King Art Center
032

The Hole
036

Vahram Muratyan
Graphic artist

French graphic artist and author of the book *Paris versus New York: A Tally of Two Cities.*

The Guggenheim
039

Alex Lin
Founder, Studio Lin

Creative director of Studio Lin. After receiving an MFA in graphic design from Yale University, Lin spent six years at the design firm 2x4.

Hugo & Marie
Creative & design agency

Founded by Jennifer Marie Gonzalez and Mario Hugo Gonzalez, Hugo & Marie represents art directors, illustrators, designers, and provides creative services for clients, studios, and brands.

The Invisible Dog Art Center
038

Chelsea Art District
040

TOMAAS
Photographer

Fashion and beauty photographer who creates cinematic, surreal yet realistic imagery that has been shown in publications and galleries worldwide.

The Met Cloisters
043

Kumi Yamashita
Artist

A Japanese-born artist who lives and works in NYC and who loves almost every minute of it!

Thomas Chen
Founder, Emmanuelle

Fashion designer and founder of NY-based fashion label Emmanuelle.

The Frick Collection
042

Film Society of Lincoln Center
044

Jay Brannan
Singer, songwriter & actor

Jay Brannan is a singer, songwriter and actor from Texas who has lived in Manhattan since 2003.

The Noguchi Museum
046

Karim Rashid
Industrial designer

A prolific designer. In his spare time Karim's pluralism flirts with art, fashion, and music and is determined to creatively touch every aspect of our physical and virtual landscape.

Julia Chiang
Artist

Loves her friends and family, making things, her dog, riding her bike, sunshine, candy, loud music, flowers, news radio, learning new things, traveling, the people and energy of NY.

Rooftop Films
045

Brooklyn Academy of Music
047

13 Storm King Art Center
Map M, P.111

Storm King is an open-air gallery with over 100 sculptural works displayed in a lovely pastoral setting located about an hour's drive (or 1.5 hours by Coach USA) from the city. Works encompass postwar periods to the present, including gifts, acquisitions and special commissions that feature site-specific large-scale sculpture, much of it in steel, as well as figurative work in stone, earth and other materials. Take a break from New York City's bustle and dedicate at least four hours to explore different areas of the art centre by foot, rental bicycle or trams for free.

🕐 1000–1730 (W–Su, Apr–Nov)
💲 $18/15/8
🏠 1 Museum Rd., New Windsor, 12553
📞 +1 (845) 534 3115
URL www.stormking.org

"*Aside from the art, there's something nice about being outdoors in open fields and woodlands. It's only open during the fair weather months.*"

– Sean Dougherty, Brand New School

14 MoMA PS1
Map K, P.110

Launched by Alanna Heiss, one of the origina-
tors of the alternative space movement in the
1970s, PS1 was known for its initiatives organis-
ing exhibitions in underutilised and abandoned
spaces across NYC. An affiliate of MoMA since
2000, MoMA PS1 has become one of the world's
leading exhibition spaces, pursuing emerging
artists, new genres and adventurous new
works by recognised artists in classroom-sized
galleries inherited from the Romanesque Re-
vival school buildings over a century old. Every
year MoMA PS1 hosts the highly anticipated
summer outdoor music series Warm Up in its
courtyard, and the NY Art Book Fair, presented
by Printed Matter, Inc., normally in September.

🕐 1200-1800 (Th-M) except Thanksgiving,
Christmas & NY   💲 $10/5
🏠 22-25 Jackson Ave., Long Island City, 11101
📞 +1 (718) 784 2084
URL www.momaps1.org

"Get there early to see the art and dance your heart
out the rest of the afternoon in the courtyard."
– Laurent Barthelemy

15 The Hole
Map B, P.105

Formerly a director at the ambitious but now-defunct Deitch Projects, artist and gallerist Kathy Grayson continues to "fill the hole in the downtown community" with her acute eye for new art. From The Hole Shop adjacent to her on-site showroom, Grayson stocks all manner of books, zines, posters and other artist products, where art publications often experiment with the conventions of reading, writing, viewing and interpretation. The space features two simultaneous exhibitions every month.

 1200–1900 (W–Su)
312 Bowery, NoHo, 10012
+1 (212) 466 1100
www.theholenyc.com

"It's right next to my studio so it's dead easy to pop in and get a beer at openings. Keep your eye on the artists they show, they'll be the next big things."

– Craig Redman, Craig & Karl

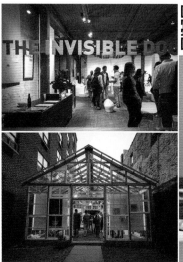

16 The Invisible Dog Art Center
Map F, P.108

Neither a commercial gallery nor a con-
cept-driven non-profit, The Invisible Dog
Art Center functions in a former factory
building built in 1863 and reopened in 2009. The
2,800sqm site offers a playground for artists to
realise site-specific experimentation and collaborations, resulting in powerful and unique
projects encompassing interdisciplinary
installations and artistic live performances.
There is always a cool mix of artists showing
their art on the ground floor and creating art
on the top-floors of this vast converted factory
building. The basement is dedicated to live
performance and special events.

🕓 1300–1900 (Th–Sa), –1700 (Su)
🏠 51 Bergen St. (b/w Smith & Court St.),
Boerum Hill, 11201
📞 +1 (347) 560 3641
URL www.theinvisibledog.org
🖉 Tu–W: By appointment only

*"Don't miss the opening nights, always
surprising and inspiring events."*
– Vahram Muratyan

17 The Guggenheim

Map K, P.110

Founded on a substantial body of Impressionist, Post-Impressionist and early modern art, Solomon R. Guggenheim Museum is at once a vital cultural centre, an educational institution and the heart of the global museum network. Frank Lloyd Wright's (1867-1959) inverted ziggurat winding pyramid design was a breakthrough in museum entrance design at the time, and was used to disperse large crowds that infuriated the architect. The spiral interior offers a continouous space and an open rotunda that affords a view of artwork on several levels at the same time.

🕐 1000-1745 (F, Su-W), -1945 (Sa)
💲 $25/18/pay-what-you-wish (Sa: 1745-1945)
🏠 1071 5th Ave. (at 89th St.), Upper East Side, 10128
📞 +1 (212) 423 3500 URL www.guggenheim.org
📎 Daily public tours: 1400

"Best to go on a weekday, it gets super crowded on weekends."

– Alex Lin, Studio Lin

18 Chelsea Art District
Map A, P.102

The Chelsea galleries are the heart of New York's contemporary art scene. With free entry to over 200 established and new galleries within a 6-block radius, this district is a convenient dossier of the city's artists and provides a very accessible way to discover and experience art, old and new, during one visit. More into design? Cooper Hewitt, Smithsonian Design Museum could be the place. Plan ahead and check gallery schedules to avoid disappointment as most galleries in New York City are closed in summer and on Sundays.

🏠 W. 18th-29th St. (around. 10th & 11th Ave.), Chelsea, Manhattan, 10001 & 10011

"You won't like everything you see here, but you're not supposed to."
– Hugo & Marie

19 The Frick Collection
Map J, P.110

The Frick Collection is open for public view in a former Henry Clay Frick (1849–1919) mansion built in the early 1900s. Reckoned as a great piece of art itself, the art museum houses a small but impressive collection of old master paintings, European sculpture and decorative arts, assembled by the industrial magnate, including masterpieces by Bellini, Rembrandt, Vermeer, Gainsborough, Goya and Whistler. Adjacent to the museum is the Frick Art Reference Library, founded in 1920 by Helen Clay Frick as a memorial to her father.

🕐 1000–1800 (Tu–Sa), 1100–1700 (Su)
💲 $22/17/12/Pay-what-you-wish (W: 1400–1800)
🏠 1 E. 70th St., Lenox Hill, 10021
📞 +1 (212) 288 0700   URL www.frick.org
🖉 Ages 10+; 1st Fridays free (1800–2100) except Sep & Jan

"If you are interested in art and architecture, this should be your number one place to visit in New York City. Art lovers will drool in this place."
– TOMAAS

20 The Met Cloisters
Map O, P.111

The Cloisters is a branch of The Metropolitan Museum of Art (The Met) devoted to medieval European art and architecture. Gardens, plantings and architectural elements are drawn from medieval Catalan, Occitan and French monasteries. With a spectacular hilltop view of the Hudson River, the building evokes a foreign setting in the northernmost quarters of Manhattan. The Cloisters collection contains sculptures, stained glass, paintings, manuscript illumination and tapestries, including the renowned Unicorn Tapestries, largely created in Western Europe.

🕐 Daily: 1000-1715 (Mar-Oct), -1645 (Nov-Feb)
💲 $25/17/12 🏠 99 Margaret Corbin Dr., Fort Tryon Park, 10040 📞 +1 (212) 923 3700
🔲 www.metmuseum.org/visit/met-cloisters
🎧 Free gallery talks: 1200, 1400 (Sa & 1st Su)

"It's a place of quiet contemplation and enchantment. Make time to just enjoy sitting in the courtyard in the sun."

– Kumi Yamashita

21 Film Society of Lincoln Center
Map J, P.110

Best known for producing the world-famous New York Film Festival and New Directors/New Films festival, the Film Society is one of the 11 resident organisations at the Lincoln Center for the Performing Arts. New films, retrospectives and archives show year round, with choices of mainstream, arthouse and avant-garde movies produced locally and around the world. The Film Society's programmes are often run at Elinor Bunin Munroe Film Center and the Walter Reade Theater on 144 and 165 W. 65th Street.

🕐 30 mins before 1st screening till 15 mins after starting the last show
💲 Ticket price varies with shows
🏠 144 & 165 W. 65th St., Manhattan, 10023 📞 +1 (212) 875 5610
URL www.filmlinc.org

"Great programmes to catch those rare-release films. Check the online schedule."

– Thomas Chen, Emmanuelle

22 Rooftop Films

Rooftop Films is a not-for-profit film festival that screens underground films and shorts in outdoor locations. Often preceded by live music, Rooftop Films events might also provide free popcorn and a bar service. Founded by curator-filmmaker Mark Elijah Rosenberg in 1997, Rooftop Films also champions independent film production by teaching filmmaking and renting equipment to artists at low-cost. Rooftop Films' Summer Series runs yearly from May or June through August or September. Regular venues include Coney Island Beach and Town Hall.

🕐 🏠 *Showtime & venues vary with programmes*
📞 *+1 (718) 417 7362*
URL *www.rooftopfilms.com*

"*Open Road Rooftop at 360 Grand street is particularly impressive. The ex-high school has amazing views of Manhattan, and stunning graffiti murals all around.*"

– Jay Brannan

23 The Noguchi Museum
Map L, P.111

Established by Isamu Noguchi (1904-88) himself and run by the Isamu Noguchi Foundation, The Noguchi Museum manages the world's most extensive collection of the artist's sculptures, architectural models, stage designs, drawings, furniture and lamps today, as well as his complete archives. The Japanese-American artist also translated his vision into the design of his own museum, which opened in 1985, to display what he deemed essential to his life's work. While the ground-floor galleries and an open-air garden presents a permanent exhibition organised by Noguchi himself, the upper floor features a rotating programme that offers studies of the artist's work in a richer context.

🕐 1000-1700 (W-F), 1100-1800 (Sa-Su) except
Thanksgiving, Christmas & NY
💲 $10/5/Free 1st Fridays
🏠 9-01 33rd Rd., Long Island City, 11106
📞 +1 (718) 204 7088 URL www.noguchi.org
✏ Free talks (EN/JP): 1400 (W-Su)

"It is a real paradise of organic sculptures, he was always inspiring to me, and this is a real hidden gem in New York."

– Karim Rashid

24 Brooklyn Academy of Music

Map F, P.108

BAM is an off-Broadway multi-arts centre and cultural icon of New York City. For more than 150 years, the institute has presented thousands of programmes that encompass dance, music, opera, film, theatre with performances as varied as an Edward Scissorhands ballet, a Jeff Mangum acoustic performance, and Sufjan Stevens instrumental light-extravaganza, The Planets. Of three main buildings scattered around the neighbourhood of Fort Greene, Peter Jay Sharp Building is the oldest, designed by architects Herts & Tallant in 1908 to contain a large opera house.

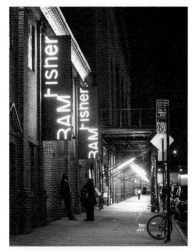

🕑 Showtime varies with programmes
🏠 Peter Jay Sharp & Box Office: 30 Lafayette Ave. / Harvey Theater: 651 Fulton St. / Fisher: 321 Ashland Pl., Brooklyn, 11217
📞 +1 (718) 636 4100 🔗 www.bam.org

"Their live shows sell out fast so if you see something you're into, go for it. If you are going to see a movie, try to see something on the main screen."

– Julia Chiang

Markets & Shops

Local designs, international finds and street food

There's only one sure way to avoid going broke in New York City and that is to leave your credit cards at home! If you're into beautiful little things, check out the historic Tender Buttons (#35) for their richly diverse, often exquisitely crafted button collections; Top Hat NYC (*245 Broome St., Lower East Side, 10002*) and Matter (#27) for a delight-inducing array of desk and studio accouterments; the Chelsea Flea Market (#25) and Brooklyn Flea (#33) for obscure memorabilia and delicious local food. For your wardrobe, find European and US indie brands at Creatures of Comfort (*205 Mulberry St., Nolita, 10012*), weekend clothing at Saturdays NYC (#38), and don't forget to shop for New York labels like Proenza Schouler, Alexander Wang or Derek Lam. Looking for something strange and unconventional? How about fancy books, magazines and unusual reads? Pay a visit to Strand Book Store (#32), Printed Matter (*231 11th Ave., Chelsea, 10001*), or Bookmarc by Marc Jacobs (*400 Bleecker St., West Village, 10014*), where purchase possibilities are endless. At the end of a busy shopping day try a no-frills tradition and sweat it out at the Russian & Turkish Baths. Closes at 10pm and opens all year round.

Greg Armas
Founder, Assembly New York

Gallery curator turned retailer and designer. Moved from LA to NYC five years ago. Stays up till 3am every night because of New York.

Johnson Trading Gallery 055

Willy Wong
CCO, NYC & Company

As NYC's CCO, I've had the privilege to collaborate on fantastic projects, with amazing partners, for the world's most exciting city, New York. Ping me @wwong

Roanne Adams
Founder, RoAndCo Studio

Adams attended Parsons School of Design and worked for Wolff Olins before starting RoAndCo in 2006. She now lives in Brooklyn with her husband Johnny and daughter Phaedra.

Chelsea Flea Market 054

Matter 056

Apartment One
Creative agency

We work intimately with clients to give truth, presence, and power to their brands. We find strength in creative partnerships and passion in the service of a greater good.

Desert Island 059

Chris Golden
Designer

Designer specialising in collage, illustration, video and installation work. He currently freelances and works with Cartoon Network / Adult Swim.

Juliana Sohn
Photographer

A photographer and a mom who loves to make things with her hands. She appreciates good food in lovely settings with good company.

Cloak & Dagger 058

Jill Platner 060

Mike Joyce
Founder, Stereotype Design

Founder of Stereotype Design. I live and work in the West Village of NYC and refuse to design wedding invitations.

Strand Book Store 063

Yuko Shimizu
Illustrator

Japanese illustrator who has been in NY for 15+ years. She teaches at School of Visual Arts and walks everywhere with her dog Bruiser. Favourite pastime is world travel.

Tara McPherson
Gallerist, Cotton Candy Machine

I create fine art paintings, rock posters, illustrations, art toys and more and I love the diversity in what I do – it keeps me excited about making art every day.

Powerhouse @ The Archway 062

Brooklyn Flea 064

Manuel Garza
Co-founder, et al. collaborative

Also an adjunct professor of architecture and design at New York Institute of Technology. Originally from Texas, via Detroit, Garza has lived in Brooklyn for about ten years.

Tender Buttons 066

Craig Ward
Art director

British designer and art director of The Words are Pictures Studio, primarily known for his typographic works which have frequently been documented and featured in publications and exhibitions globally.

MOGOLLON
Multimedia creative agency

Founders Monica Brand and Francisco Lopez focus on creating visionary imagery for art, film, music and fashion clients globally. "Mogollon" is Spanish slang word for "plenty."

Crest Hardware 065

Acme Smoked Fish 067

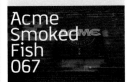

25 Chelsea Flea Market
Map A, P.102

Every weekend, year round, this alleyway next to the 150-year-old Trinity Chapel Complex transforms into a busy vintage treasure hunting ground with over a hundred vendors selling everything from old milk caps to mid-century furniture. Many were tenants of the now closed Antique Garage. Talk to them and ask questions. You'll be surprised with what they've seen and whom they've met during their time at the garage. More furniture can be found at "sister flea", Hell's Kitchen Flea Market, running the block of 39th street between 9th and 10th Avenues.

🕑 0630-1800 (Sa-Su) 💲 $1
🏠 W. 25th St. (b/w 6th Ave. & Broadway), Chelsea, 10010 📞 +1 (212) 243 5343
🔗 annexmarkets.com/chelsea-flea-market

"Fun collection of European antiques and characters. Good conversation will get you better deals than haggling here."

– Greg Armas, Assembly New York

26 Johnson Trading Gallery
Map N, P.111

Established as a forum to produce and exhibit significant industrial design projects, the gallery has a full rotation of exhibitions displaying works by established and new architects, designers and artists, as well as highlighting major historical design movements. Just recently, founder Paul Johnson relocated his space from Tribeca to the former 1940s theater in Queens to showcase his trove of vintage and uber contemporary furniture designs, which invite touch and play. His vast collection of work by Robert Loughlin (1949–2011) is essential to see.

🏠 47/42 43rd St., Woodside, 11377
📞 +1 (212) 925 1110
🔗 johnsontradinggallery.com
🔗 By appointment only

*"Take the 7 train to 40th street.
While you're out there you might as well grab a bite
at SriPraPhai, just 4 stops east on the 7."*

– Willy Wong, NYC & Company

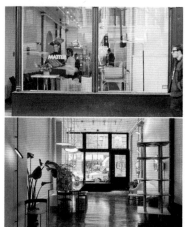

27 Matter
Map B, P.104

With an ultramodern catalog of lighting and furniture to jewelry and wallpaper, Matter is not only a design shop, but a gallery, showroom and manufacturer all in one. Their singular vision usually involves very current and often local furniture and object designers often not found in other design stores, luring in architects and interior designs in quest of effortlessly stylish home décor. Matter collaborates and connects deeply with the design community, so expect to see pieces by takemakers such as Fort Standard, Bec Brittain and Jonah Takagi.

🕙 1000–1800 (M–F), by appointment only (Sa)
🏠 405 Broome St., Nolita, 10013
📞 +1 (212) 343 2600 URL mattermatters.com

"Make sure to check out Matter-Made, the shop's signature collection of lighting and furniture."

– Roanne Adams, RoAndCo Studio

28 Cloak & Dagger
Map B, P.105

Starting her own clothing label Cloak & Dagger in 2006 with an urge to create clothes that were fun and comfortable yet chic and refined, designer Brookelynn Starnes conveys her vision and sense of tailoring with inventive juxtapositioning, intimate detailing, patterns and luxury fabrics. With an outpost in trendy East Village, Cloak & Dagger carries quality ladies' brands and vintage cuts from across the globe. Look for regular stock updates on the web and visit her store to try them for real.

🕐 1200-2000 (M-F), 1100- (Sa), 1100-1900 (Su)
🏠 334 E. 9th St., East Village, 10003
📞 +1 (212) 673 0500
URL cloakanddaggernyc.com

"You'll find the best clothing curation of designer and vintage items. Say 'hi' to Brookelynn!"
– Apartment One

29 Desert Island

Map I, P.109

Desert Island is in fact a colourful comic and art world chock-full of art prints, zines, comics and posters for all kinds of tastes. Their well-curated selection highlights established, budding and underground artists, illustrators and designers from the States and beyond. As often as not you can find old classics, back issues and rare prints which you'll have a hard time finding anywhere else. Look for *Smoke Signal*, the shop's own free quarterly comics tabloid which invites a different body of talents to contribute to its content and cover art.

🕐 1200–2100 (M–Sa), –1900 (Su)
🏠 540 Metropolitan Ave., Williamsburg, 11211
📞 +1 (718) 388 5087
🔗 www.desertislandbrooklyn.com

"Awesome little comic and art shop! If you love music, or more specifically dance music, check out the Fools Gold Record Store next door."

– Chris Golden

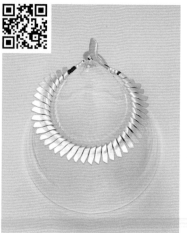

30 **Jill Platner**
Map B, P.104

A true artist at heart, Jill Platner has dedicated herself to nearly three decades of hand-crafting jewelry in New York. Her taste is for urban-artsy luxe, much in the minimalistic vein of aesthetics inspired by both organic and urban forms but speaks volume on the body, in sterling silver and 19K gold. Refined and covetable, every precious piece displayed around the airy showroom are meticulously made with a skilled team of artisans above the shop. There's something for (almost) everyone, even the home.

🕐 1200–1800 (M-Su)
🏠 113 Crosby St., SoHo, 10012
📞 +1 (212) 324 1298
URL www.jillplatner.com

"Try the jewelry on. It comes alive on the body and you'll love something you never would have chosen from a photo."

– Juliana Sohn

31 Powerhouse @ The Archway
Map C, P.107

Powerhouse @ The Archway boasts soaring 24-
foot ceilings, amphitheatre-style seating and
spacious ground floor, but only there are also
shelves of books with the cool worlds of art,
photography, design, and fashion. Established
by the powerHouse Books, this raw open space
is especially known for their literary events,
regular book release parties and readings that
attract audiences from everywhere. Try to
catch one of their landmark exhibitions and
performances too after browsing. If you're
after timeless dandy goods, check out Modern
Anthology nearby on Jay Street.

🕐 1100-1900 (M-F), -1800 (Sa, Su)
🏠 28 Adams St., Brooklyn, 11201
✆ +1 (718) 666 3049
URL www.powerhousearena.com

"*Spend some time walking around DUMBO. It's a
great area of Brooklyn with amazing views of the
Brooklyn Bridge and Manhattan skyline.*"
– Mike Joyce, Stereotype Design

32 Strand Book Store
Map B, P.105

Unlike the usual familiar chains you know, Strand Book Store is a local business and home to "18 miles of books" that are loved, reasonably-priced, and cover topics as far-ranging as occult to philosophy to finance. Opened in 1927 by Ben Bass on Fourth Avenue, what was then called "Book Row" and housed 48 bookstores, the Strand is the last store remaining and is now run by Bass' son and granddaughter, with knowledgeable staff who are happy and able to recommend books according to customers' literary tastes. Rare Book Room (RBR) is a salon of aged proofs, first editions and signed books, open to public and renting for events.

🕐 0930–2230 (M–Sa), 1100– (Su)
🏠 828 Broadway (& 12th St.), Manhattan, 10003
📞 +1 (212) 473 1452
🔗 www.strandbooks.com
✏ RBR: 0930–1815 (Mo–Sa), 1100– (Su)

"This is a bookstore every artist, designer and art student flock to. Shop a lot with confidence! They also have a very inexpensive international shipping :-)"

– Yuko Shimizu

33 Brooklyn Flea
Map C / Map E, P.107

From obscure memorabilia, classic vinyls, and vintage clothing to handmade goodies and local designer ware for both the chic and the eclectic, the Brooklyn Flea is a fun place to find souvenirs and surprises. Even though the market's location varies depending on the season, it is also the perfect point from which to explore the surrounding neighbourhoods and soak in the charming vibes of Brooklyn. Tired after hours of bargain hunting? Fuel up with coffee and a bite or two from one of the many vendors offering tasty F&B options.

🕙 1000–1700
🏠 241 37th St., 11232 (Apr–Oct: Sa, Nov–Mar: Sa- Su), 80 Pearl St., 11201 (Apr–Oct: Su)
URL brooklynflea.com

"While you shop for that cool handmade item, enjoy yummy food and the view of Manhattan. "
– Tara McPherson

34 Crest Hardware

Map I, P.109

Sited in the heart of Williamsburg, Crest Hardware has grown from a family business with a pet parrot and everything you need for art projects, to a community that shares a love for creative art. Every summer, owner Joe Franquinha co-produces and curates Crest Fest and The Crest Hardware Art Show where local and overseas artists flock to showcase their hardware-inspired artwork. Crest Fest always draws an avid throng with a lineup of DJs, a live music stage and a vendor market offering beers, food and handmade crafts.

🕒 0800–1900 (M–F), 0800– (Sa), 1000–1700 (Su) 🏠 558 Metropolitan Ave., Williamsburg, 11211
📞 +1 (718) 388 9521
🔗 cresthardwarenyc.com

"Go in the summer when the hardware store turns into a venue for local art and music."

– Manuel Garza, et al. collaborative

35 Tender Buttons
Map A, P.103

Since the late Diana Epstein acquired her button shop in 1964 on a whim, revived it with the name of a 1914 book by Gertrude Stein, and formed a partnership with the shop's current owner Millicent Safro, Tender Buttons has become a button museum and Mecca for button collectors, fashion éclat and crafters. The tiny brick townhouse is adorable with drawers upon labelled drawers of glass, brass, porcelain and plastic buttons in every thinkable style, size and shape. The store retains as the only place devoted solely to buttons in the States.

🕐 1030–1800 (M-F), –1730 (Sa)
🏠 143 E. 62nd St., Lenox Hill, 10065
📞 +1 (212) 758 7004
URL www.tenderbuttons-nyc.com

"My wife took me here a long time ago and it cemented in my mind why I love NYC. Grab crostini and a glass of wine at Fig & Olive nearby and feel ever so grown up."
– Craig Ward, The Words are Pictures Studio

36 Acme Smoked Fish
Map I, P.109

Since it opened business in 1954 by Harry Brownstein and his sons, Acme has been one of Brooklyn's best kept secrets and a great place for any food lover to explore. Now run by fourth generation family members, Acme remains a dedicated supplier of first-rate fruitwood-smoked products to local stores, and directly to the masses on "Fish Fridays" through their factory, where customers get to venture inside the workroom and choose from a beautiful array of smoked fish. Specialties span salmon, trout, mackerel and herring.

🕐 0800–1300 (F)
📍 30 Gem St., Greenpoint, 11222
📞 +1 (718) 383 8585
URL www.acmesmokedfish.com
🏷 Cash only

"Going there is an amazing and very local experience. Ask kindly for Salmon Belly."

– MOGOLLON

HOT DRINKS

Stumptown Drip Coffee
Sm 2.45   Med 2.75   Lg 3.10

Whole Beans
15/bag

Organic Tea (earl grey, oolong, Sencha & Peppermint)
Sm 2.45   Med 2.75   Lg 3.10

Belloco Tea of the Month
*Market Price

COLD DRINKS

Stumptown Cold Brew
Sm 3.75   Lg 3.95

Ginger Hibiscus Iced Tea
2.75

Housemade Lemonade
3.85

Brooklyn Barn Almond Milk
Shot 1.50   Sm 3.20   Lg 3.75

Organic Local Milk
Sm 2.00   Lg 3.55

Restaurants & Cafés

Modern classics, ethnic food and exquisite cakes

Be prepared to leave the city with a few extra pounds from its food! Having been one of the world's most favoured migrant destinations for centuries, there's nowhere quite like eating in New York City, a place which celebrates diversity and culture through food. Ask local residents Julia Chiang or Braulio Amado, and a never-ending list of places rolls off the tongue. Places like Midtown for Shake Shack (burgers), Lower East Side for Economy Candy *(108 Rivington St., 10002)* and Babycakes NYC *(248 Broome St., 10002)*, Chinatown for veggie meals and dumplings, West Village for Joe's Pizza (#42) and Julius' *(159 W. 10th St., 10014)*, Williamsburg for The Meatball Shop *(170 Bedford Ave., 11249)*, Dumbo for a cheap lunch, Long Island City for Court Square Diner's curly fries *(45-30 23rd St., 11101)*... and for an international menu, everyone says Smorgasburg (#45) and Essex Street Market *(120 Essex St., Lower East Side, 10002)* for fresh produce and gourmet cheese. From sweet to savoury, brunch to dinner and coffee breaks in between, this section epitomises the fact that quality food can be had at any budget, at any hour, in every neighbourhood, and is often full of surprises. Also get a life-changing experience with Super Heebster Sandwich at Russ & Daughters *(179 E. Houston St., Lower East Side, 10002)*. Late-night lifesavers with oyster plates can also be found in Nightlife.

Sophia Chang
Artist

Hails from Queens and works in all mediums of crafted matter. In her spare time she enjoys frolicking through the park with her dog and giving him unconditional love.

Saturdays NYC 073

Base NYC
Design agency

Base NYC. Your strategy. Your identity. Your personality. We grow potential.

SITU Studio
Architectural firm

An architecture and research practice committed to inter-disciplinary collaborations and founded in 2005 while its four partners were studying archi-tecture at the Cooper Union.

Caffe Reggio 072

Julia Pott
Animator & illustrator

British animator and illustrator living in Brooklyn. When she is not drawing she is usually peo-ple watching and consuming large amounts of sugar and caffeine.

Buddha Bodai Kosher Vegetarian Restaurant 076

Jon Burgerman
Artist

Burgerman is a British born artist now living in Brooklyn. He draws and paints, scratches and scrawls, sleeps and bawls.

Brooklyn Roasting Company 074

Eric Wrenn
Art director

Eric Wrenn is a New York–based art director working with cli-ents in the creative industry.

Ovenly 075

Joe's Pizza 077

Deanne Cheuk & Chris Rubino, *Artists*

Deanne Cheuk and Chris Rubino both create art and work in art direction and illustration. Deanne is represented by Hugo & Marie and Chris is represented by Art Department.

Pier 66 Maritime Bar & Grill 079

Tyler Hopf
Architect & designer

A young architect and designer in New York City.

Kelli Anderson
Artist & graphic designer

A New Orleanian-turned New Yorker living in Brooklyn with her other half, two cats, one 1919 letterpress, five computers and a couple hundred books.

Macaron Parlour 078

Smorgasburg 080

Rus Anson
Fashion photographer

A photographer from Barcelona living in Brooklyn. Through photography, Anson creates fantastic, surreal and naive worlds often inspired by her imagination and daydreams.

Chuko 082

Jennifer Daniel
Designer & editor

Designer, writer and editor. When not working as the graphic director at Bloomberg BusinessWeek she can be found in a bar drinking beer after a long bike ride.

Peter Sluszka
Film director

Specialising in mixed media and animation, I work in film, music videos, commercials, and live projection. NYC's energy and constant reinvention still surprises and inspires me.

House of Small Wonder 081

Roberta's 083

37 Caffe Reggio
Map B, P.104

Find one of the world's oldest espresso machines at Caffe Reggio, proudly one of the first to have served cappuccino in the States. Made in 1902, the machine symbolises the café's rich history as taste pioneers since 1927. Located right by Washington Square Park and New York University, the quiet, small coffee place makes for a nice spot to sip an "Original Cappuccino" while relaxing and watching people on their antique bench, once owned by the illustrious Medici family in Italy. The café occasionally runs poetry nights and has made a movie appearance in *Inside Llewyn Davis* (2013).

🕘 0900-0300 (Su-Th), -4000 (Fr, Sa)
📍 119 Macdougal St., Greenwich Village 10012
📞 +1 (212) 475 9557 f @Caffe Reggio

"Their dishes are small but appetising. Stop by for a quick coffee and enjoy the space!"
– Sophia Chang

38 Saturdays NYC
Map B, P.104

As well as products and surrounds that make for a stylish interpretation of East Coast surfer cool slap bang in the city, Saturdays NYC brews java with well-loved La Colombe brand coffees directly acquired from Gera (Ethiopia), Finisterre Mountains (Papua New Guinea), Haiti and Tarrazu (Costa Rica) for an unforgettably dense and unique flavour – whether it comes as an espresso or drip. Make yourself comfortable in their cosy courtyard, and be sure you flip through the books near the entrance too. There's always something special to discover.

🕐 1000-1900 daily, Coffee Bar: 0800-1900 (M-F), 1000- (Sa, Su)
📍 31 Crosby St., SoHo, 10013
📞 +1 (212) 966 7875
🔗 saturdaysnyc.com

"Great coffee, great people, great backyard. We stop in at least twice a day. Order an iced RedEye on a hot summer day (or all year round)."
– Base NYC

Base

39 Brooklyn Roasting Company
Map C, P.107

Brooklyn Roasting Company's "coffeeloso-phy" is to offer best quality fair trade, organic and Rainforest Alliance-certified coffees and espressos. Beans are roasted in-house on a Loring Kestrel 1/2 bag roaster, and the owners have devised their own tasting scale. The cafe serves pure espressos as well as iced lattes made from an espresso of your choice, while an espresso lab offers private cuppings by appointment and courses in brewing espresso-based drinks.

🕐 0700-1900 daily
🏠 25 Jay St., Dumbo, 11201
📞 +1 (718) 855 1000
URL brooklynroasting.com

"On-premises roasting of fair trade coffee and local baked goods like Dough's doughnuts from Bed-stuy."

– SITU Studio

40 Ovenly
Map I, P.109

Named "Best New Bakery" in Time Out's New York Food and Drink Awards in 2013, Ovenly is a creative kitchen and coffee shop run by baking aficionados Agatha Kulaga and Erin Patinkin, who met at a food-focused book club. It appears magic arises between flour and ovens as the duo works to innovate traditional Eastern European recipes and re-create favourite breakfast pastries, desserts and snacks. Aside from the shop, the historic area is often used for movie locations and is brilliant for walking off your sugar fix.

🕐 0730-1900 (M-F), 0800- (Sa-Su)
🏠 31 Greenpoint Ave., Greenpoint, 11222 📞 +1 (888) 899 2213
🔗 www.oven.ly

"Get the Salted Chocolate Chip Cookie or the Jelly Donut Muffin, and take your delicious treats to the park by the water or peruse the shops on Franklin street."

– Julia Pott

41 Buddha Bodai Kosher Vegetarian Restaurant

Map C, P.106

Wander to Chinatown's main street for an authentic taste of Chinese cuisine, veggie-style. Buddha Bodai offers an extensive selection of classic Chinese dishes that feature "meat" replicated using tofu, bean curd, gluten, eggs and konjac with flavoured sauces, catering to vegetarians, vegans, ovo-lacto vegetarians and kosher. Most dishes are available as bite-sized dim sum plates or in sharing portions and it's common to share your table with strangers as demand for space grows.

🕐 1100-2130 (M-F), 1000- (Sa, Su)
🏠 5 Mott St., Chinatown, 10013
📞 +1 (212) 566 8388
URL buddha-bodai.com

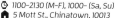

"Get the Sesame Chicken Balls. I didn't know chickens have balls, especially non-meat-pretend chickens, but they do and they are tasty."

– Jon Burgerman

🕐 1000–0400 (Su–Th), –0500 (F–Sa)
🏠 7 Carmine St., Greenwich Village, 10014
📞 +1 (212) 366 1182
🔗 joespizzanyc.com

42 Joe's Pizza
Map B, P.104

Ask any native New Yorker for the definition of authentic pizza, and many will point you to Joe's Pizza at 7 Carmine street. Widely recognised as "the quintessential New York slice," the classic pizza joint, after nearly 40 years in business, insists on re-creating the true Italian flavours based on simple, quality ingredients introduced by founder Joe Pozzuoli, who migrated from Naples, Italy to the States. Grab a bite as "late" as five in the morning and discover fancy toppings are not at all necessary for a good slice of pizza.

"Joe's Pizza in the West Village is essential."

– Eric Wrenn

🕐 0730-1915 (M-F), 0830- (Sa, Su)
🏠 44 Hester St. (b/w Essex & Ludlow), 10002
📞 +1 (212) 387 9169
URL macaronparlour.com

43 Macaron Parlour
Map C, P.107

Owners Christina Ha and Simon Tung have a strong macaron pedigree. Ha developed her love for the bite-sized petit fours studying macarons at La Haute Pâtisserie Pierre Hermé in Paris, while Tung perfected his macaron technique with award-winning chef Stephane Glacier. The result is Macaron Parlour, which opened in 2010 to expand macaron offerings beyond traditional fillings and offers inventive flavours such as Honey & Cognac, Cheetos and Candied Bacon with Maple Cream Cheese – all of them taste absurdly satisfying! The patisserie also serves a variety of baked goods along with teas and drinks.

"Stop by for some Blue Bottle Coffee, and all the macarons you can eat... don't forget to check out the art wall!"

– Deanne Cheuk & Chris Rubino

44 Pier 66 Maritime Bar & Grill
Map A, P.102

Frying Pan is a historic vessel-turned-floating bar that had spent three years under water before being salvaged. Offering an unbeatable view of the Hudson River and New York's skyline, it forms part of Pier 66 Maritime Bar & Grill's dining setting, where tables are available on a first come, first served basis. Arriving early might guarantee you a favourable spot, but the place is even better at dusk with a cooling pitcher of drink, as the sunset glows over the water – a perfect respite after a long day of travel. Order your food and drink at the bar, a buzzer will alert you when your food is ready to retrieve from the kitchen window.

🕐 1200–0000 daily weather permitting, except Nov–Mar
🏠 Pier 66, W. 26th St. & West Side Highway, Hudson River Park, 10001   📞 +1 (212) 989 6363
🔗 pier66maritime.com

"Grab a beer, a burger and sit on the very end to enjoy the breeze, watch ships drive by, and hear the water hitting the pier."

– Tyler Hopf

45 Smorgasburg

Every Saturday morning during the warmer months, little booths set up on the Williamsburg waterfront (or at Brooklyn Bridge Park (#2) on Sundays) to sell homemade foodstuffs to the masses. While the list of purveyors and vendors might vary by year, there will likely always be a family that makes homemade Greek yogurt with sour cherries, ice pops from seasonal local fruits, Colombian arepas, fish tacos, homemade kimchi, spiced nuts, and virtually anything else your taste buds desire and all from the nicest business vendors imaginable. Check to see if Smorgasburg is running its indoor market during a winter visit. It did in 2013.

🕐 1100–1800 (Apr–Oct), 1000–1700 (Nov–Mar) 🏠 Prospect Park (Apr–Oct: Su), 90 Kent Ave., 11211 (Apr–Oct: Sa), , 241 37th St., 11232 (Nov–Mar: Sa & Su)
URL smorgasburg.com

"I once bought a tomato soup here from a member of Vampire Weekend (and his soup-chef girlfriend). Get there by 11am (or go late) to avoid the masses."

– Kelli Anderson

46 House of Small Wonder
Map I, P.109

Easily passed by, the little café's plain planked wood store front and small entrance actually leads to a delightful interior where its quiet, relaxing vibe transports you back to grandma's porch. Serving homemade soups, fresh salads, and great coffee as well as sandwiches, croissants and other pastries at reasonable prices, the café mixes cosy breakfast and lunch gatherings with a Japanese touch. A young ash tree inside the restaurant blends perfectly with the navy wallpaper, wooden tables, innumerable potted plants and cute artworks. A sun-infused greenhouse warms a Japanese forest.

🕘 0900–1800 (M-Th), –1730 (F), 1000– (Sa), –1700 (Su)   🏠 77 N. 6th St., Williamsburg, 11211
📞 +1 (718) 388 6160
🔗 houseofsmallwonder.com

"Three words: Banana-Nutella Croissant."

– Rus Anson

47 Chuko
Map G, P.108

If the heart of any good bowl of ramen is its broth, Chuko serves diners big and warm hugs from the inside with rich and hearty flavours that are anything but overpowering. Its unique interiors are a comforting mix of Japanese working-class bar meets unpretentious Brooklyn grit, making it a welcoming pit stop after a full day of exploring. While the restaurant is also known for its non-ramen fare like its shrimp buns and okonomiyaki-style tater tots, vegetarians will be in for a treat as its meat-free menu comes highly recommended.

🕙 1200-1500 daily, 1730-2200 (Su-Th), -2300 (F-Sa) 🏠 565 Vanderbilt Ave., Brooklyn, 11238
📞 +1 (347) 425 9570
URL chukobk.com

"Eat it all."
– Jennifer Daniel

48 Roberta's

Map D, P.107

Farm to table done Brooklyn style – because the farm is just next door, where homegrown cherries and berries, beets and flowers colour up the otherwise bland building. Roberta's menu is simple, delicious and eclectic, with brick-oven-baked pizzas, grilled produce and seafood characterised by unexpected textures and flavours. Their gelato is another standout, available in all kinds of seasonal flavours. Walk-in-only policy means going later than 5pm can lead to a two-hour wait. For a more upscale experience, make a reservation for the tasting menu at Blanca, an offshoot of Roberta's at the same location.

🕐 1100-1600 (M-F), 1000- (Sa, Su), 1600-0000 daily
🏠 261 Moore St., Williamsburg, 11206 📞 +1 (718) 417 1118
🔗 robertaspizza.com

"The Bushwick neighbourhood is full of young artists, so check out some galleries to see what's fresh while working up an appetite."

– Peter Sluszka

Bossa Nova
CIVIC CLUB

Drafts $6

* PACIFICO
* LAGUNITAS IPA
* BITBURGER
* STELLA
* SWEET ACTION
* BROWNSTONE
* ABITA AMBER
* HOEGARDEN

$9

IMBA JALAPENO /CILANT...
ED JIMADOR TEQUILA, HONEY
, CINNAMON

GO
S VODKA, WATERMELON, LIME,
Y

ND
DRICKS GIN, PIMM S, CUCUMBER,
N, MINT

NOVA SMASH
OVERHOLT RYE, LEMON, MIN

GAY
OGURT R M, PINK
S

Nightlife

Wild parties, club nights and original cocktails

Wake up in the city that never sleeps, as Frank Sinatra wished, and you are sure to catch New York City's metropolitan glam and delirium. Lights and music take over the traffic-filled streets at night, and whether you're a hands-in-the-air clubber or *New York, New York* jazz enthusiast, there's always somewhere to spend the night (and, often, early morning) revelling. Find out where the party's at with travelling collective CHERYL (#55), or enter The Box (#53) for a taste of renaissance prohibition-era cocktails complete with showgirls. To enjoy Manhattan's remarkable cityscape, pick one of the rooftop lounges in this section or go for a stroll along the water. Dumbo has one of the most beautiful views of the skyline, and a summer sunset between the Brooklyn and Manhattan bridges is stunning. Spare a night for live music. Bands play at places like Joe's Pub *(425 Lafayette St., NoHo, 10003)*, or lay down on The Dream House's floor *(275 Church St. (3F), Tribeca, 10013)* and absorb sound installations by minimalist artist/musicians La Monte Young and Marian Zazeela. Check programme schedules, book tickets or tables ahead of time if possible, and pack a strategic wardrobe to avoid being on the wrong side of the purple rope.

Reonda Cheng
Designer, Bowoo NYC

Musician and founder of Bowoo, a specialist design firm set up to supply guitar cases all made in the USA.

Fanelli Cafe
091

Moh Azima
Film director

Filmmaker living and working in NYC for 15+ years. "While this city can be hard at times, it always rewards you for your efforts."

Gerald Ding
Creative director, Psyop

Brazilian Jiu Jitsu student of Renzo Gracie, a goalkeeper for the Chinatown Soccer Club (sometimes), a vegetarian, a husband, a brother, a father to a French Bulldog named Bob.

Fat Cat
090

An Choi
092

STUDIO NEWWORK
Design agency

A graphic design studio and a team of passionate typographic designers with commitment to search for excellence in design. We design with passion, care, and love.

The Box
094

Frances Rose
Band

Sisters Sarah Frances and Michelle Rose Cagianese form Frances Rose. Classically trained, the duo has been singing and playing music together their entire lives.

Aaron Duffy
Director, 1stAveMachine

Director and creative director at 1stAveMachine. Duffy loves to crochet and has a turtle named Chevy.

Maison Premiere
093

Weather Up
095

Braulio Amado
Graphic designer & illustrator

Portuguese graphic designer and freelance illustrator who likes to play music and take photographs. Amado came to NYC in 2010 to finish his studies and worked at Pentagram NYC.

CHERYL
096

Richard Turley
Creative director

Creative director of *Bloomberg Businessweek*. Turley studied graphic art in Liverpool, UK. He worked at *The Guardian* before moving to New York to reinvent *Businessweek*.

Le Bain
099

Penthouse at Dream
097

LONG TRAN
Fashion designer

Originally from Vietnam, LONG TRAN now lives in New York City and New Jersey to pursue his dream. "Like other artists, I love to explore to get inspiration and refresh my mind."

Catfish
100

Mike Perry
Artist

Designer and artist living in Brooklyn. He is a big fan of finding the small community within a massive one.

Selebrities
Band

A Brooklyn-based four piece, lauded for their signature brand of new wave romantic pop. Material is woven around themes of emotional intimacy, sexuality and urban living.

Bossa Nova Civic Club
098

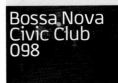

Emmanuel André
Chief Operating Officer, TBWA

Born in France and raised on two continents, André pursues an active life in photography and currently lives in NY with his wife Hong Tam and their sons, Louis and Matthieu.

Death & Co.
101

49 Fat Cat
Map B, P.104

More than just a live house with nightly music and late night jam sessions, Fat Cat is a fully-equipped gaming centre and a cool place to drink beer or soju. Pay a minimal fee for unlimited chess games, enter a foosball tournament every Tuesday night, or just scope out this spacious dive bar-slash-pool hall free of charge every Friday at 7pm. Don't worry about dressing up for the basement club, just relax and enjoy music by emerging artists and legends of jazz, latin, classical and world music. After Hours sessions close at 4am.

🕐 1400-0500 (M-Th), 1200- (F-Su)
💲 $3 (after 1800)   🏠 75 Christopher St. (at 7th Ave.), West Village, 10014   📞 +1 (212) 675 6056
🔗 fatcatmusic.org   🎫 21+ after 2200 (F-Sa)

"Go at night if you prefer a noisy fun evening, or earlier in the afternoon if you want some laid back ping pong fun."

– Reonda Cheng, Bowoo NYC

50 Fanelli Cafe
Map B, P.104

As one of the five oldest bars in the city located right in the heart of SoHo, Fanelli Cafe does not just serve beers and delicious burgers, but also a big helping of New York history. Once a speakeasy during the Prohibition from 1920 to 1933, it became a gathering place for artists from the Beat Generation era, where conversations fueled creative ideas, partnerships, and everything else in between. Its ambience retains a casual, low-key vibe from those days that makes it the perfect refuge for the nearby working class to let loose.

🕐 1000-0130 (Su-Th), -0400 (Fr, Sa)
🏠 94 Prince St., Manhattan, 10012
📞 +1 (212) 226 9412
f @Fanelli Cafe

"Try the chilli and drink the Budweiser on tap; and don't talk back to the bartender, he can be moody ;)"

– Moh Azima

51 An Choi
Map B, P.105

With its open store front, stencilled handyman
ads on the wall, and dim hanging light bulbs,
An Choi contrives a hipster version of a Ho
Chi Minh City alley at the Lower East Side of
Manhattan. Started by Tuan Bui and Huy Bui,
founder of "HB" Collaborative, the dining spot
adopts a streetside vibe and serves authentic
Vietnamese *pho* and *bánh mì* (Vietnam-
ese-style baguette) to go, with five-spiced
ham or house-made pâté. Get a Hummingbird
cocktail and hang out at their cosy bar. It's
open till late.

🕐 1800-0000 (M), 1200- (Tu-Th, Su), -0200 (F-Sa)
🏠 85 Orchard St. (b/w Broome & Grand St.),
Lower East Side, 10002   📞 +1 (212) 226 3700
URL anchoinyc.com

*"Great Vietnamese food with a home-cooked feeling.
I wish the Taro Fries came in a KFC bucket size."*
– Gerald Ding, Psyop

52 Maison Premiere
Map I, P.109

Absinthe, dim lights, and bartenders with suspenders over their white shirts all help create the mellow yet classy atmosphere of Maison Premiere. Reflective of old-fashioned good time halls in New York and New Orleans, as well as cafés in Paris, Maison Premiere is an oyster house and cocktail den that offers a dozen-plus premium absinthes. About 30 varieties of oyster fill out a seafood-focused menu with choices based on market availability. Opt for a table in the garden where vines creep and plants encircle diners surrounded by soft lights. If you're worried about choosing from such a large selection, book the chef's six-course tasting menu at least one day in advance.

🕐 1400–0200 (M–W), –0400 (Th–F), 1100–0400 (Sa), –1600 (Su)
🏠 298 Bedford Ave., Brooklyn, 11249
📞 +1 (347) 335 0446
🔗 maisonpremiere.com

"All oysters are \$1 each during Happy Hour (4–7pm, M–F)."
– STUDIO NEWWORK

53 **The Box**
Map B, P.105

Lodged in a former sign factory, The Box is a theatre, club, and cabaret lounge where risqué cabaret and burlesque shows take the stage nightly (except Mondays) starting from 1am. Run by a crew of theatrical moguls, the speakeasy-style two-storey club holds two bars and six banquettes that accommodate six to 12 guests on the ground floor together with a mezzanine floor that offers the best vantage point for outlandish vaudeville. Arrive in style no later than midnight, or 1am if you have a table reserved. No phones or cameras allowed.

🕐 2300 till late (Tu-Sa)
🏠 189 Chrystie St., Lower East Side, 10002
📞 +1 (917) 982 9301
🌐 theboxnyc.com

"It's fun. If you wanna be in, you wanna be there. Go dance. New York never sleeps."

– Frances Rose

54 Weather Up Brooklyn
Map G, P.108

The refined, mood-lit interior and little garden are just two of the signature elements that define this intimate cocktail joint. Under a subway-tiled ceiling and box-like lamps, a tight range of expertly-mixed drinks from a menu drawn up by British owner and mixologist Kathryn Weatherup lands on the copper-topped bar. Much of Weatherup's influence and skill comes from cocktail guru Sasha Petraske who runs Milk & Honey in Flatiron District, and much attention here is given to gin and the craft of ice. The bar's leather-bound barstools are designed by the team behind The Box (#53).

🕐 1730–0200 daily
🏠 589 Vanderbilt Ave., Prospect Heights, 11238
URL weatherupnyc.com

"I don't go often because it's more of a treat than a go-to. The back patio with any Weather Up drink is a perfect combo."

– Aaron Duffy, 1stAveMachine

55 CHERYL

CHERYL is a Brooklyn-based artist quartet who are frequently found out and about donning cat masks and throwing "life-ending" theme dance parties year round at clubs, party houses and museums around town. Since celebrating their fifth birthday in 2013, the fun continues. Ridiculous costumes and resident DJ Nick spinning tunes offer hints of euphoria and dollops of drama. Follow them on twitter @ CHERYLDANCE to stay in the loop. When the party is on, dress up, open your mind and go wild alongside the crazy fun crowd for the most unforgettable night in NYC.

Venue & admission vary with programmes
cherylwillruinyourlife.info 21+

"*Very NYC. Best themes, best costumes, best music, most fun people and least amount of pretentiousness. Get crazy! You'll dance your ass off.*"

– Braulio Amado

56 Penthouse at Dream
Map A, P.102

Tucked into a penthouse on the 12th floor of the luxurious Dream Downtown hotel, formerly the New York Maritime Hotel, PH-D offers from the outdoor terrace breathtaking views of the city. Inside, a lavish interior features floor-to-ceiling glass windows and a state-of-the-art sound, light and audio system. Settle in before 7pm during summer to watch the magnificent Manhattan skyline change from sunset to dusk, free of cover charge. If you want to target the celebrity and hipster crowd, show up after 9.30pm.

🕐 0800–0400 (M), 1700– (Tu-Sa), –0000 (Su)
🏠 355 W. 16th St., Chelsea, 10011
📞 +1 (212) 229 2511
URL phdlounge.com

"To go there free, dress up after 9pm."

– LONG TRAN

57 **Bossa Nova Civic Club**
Map D, P.107

The Bossa Nova Civic Club has nothing much to do with Brazilian jazz fusion. Since the tropically-themed cocktail bar and dance club began throwing late night parties in 2012 it has quickly emerged as one of New York's hottest party destinations. Techno and house music pumps at this 1800s mansion location, known as Trip House, found right under the M Train Central stop. The wildest parties happen on Fridays and Saturdays after midnight.

🕐 1700–0400 (Mo–Sa), –0000 (Su)
🏠 1271 Myrtle Ave., Bushwick, 11221
📞 +1 (718) 443 1271
📘 @Bossa Nova Civic Club

"*Free to enter, good music, drinks not too expensive. Shake your butt and live it up. On the weekends late there tends to be a line to get in.*"
– Selebrities

58 Le Bain
Map A, P.102

In the heart of the Meatpacking District, elevated above the High Line (#4), the fourth Standard hotel houses Le Bain. The penthouse disco and rooftop bar affords a 360° view of Hudson River and downtown Manhattan. A plunge pool opens on the dance floor during the summer and a crêperie serves sweet and savoury crepes with locally-sourced ingredients. Cocktails can cost an arm and a leg, or order a beer. Go in through the sidewalk entrance at the side of the hotel.

🕐 2200-0400 (W-F), 1400- (Sa), -0300 (Su)
🏠 444 W. 13th St., Manhattan, 10014
📞 +1 (212) 645 7600 URL standardhotels.com/high-line/food-drink/le-bain

"Ignore everything on the ground floor and find your way to the roof bar. The view is breathtaking and it's remarkably relaxed."
– Richard Turley, Bloomberg BusinessWeek

 Catfish
Map G, P.108

New Orleans right in the heart of Brooklyn. Catfish serves up authentic Cajun food in a rustic interior and has a backyard patio and a decent selection of rye, scotch and fine spirits. The place is founded by three bartender-friends who have been mixing drinks on the scene for years. Although you can still go for weekend brunch or happy hour specials (4.30-7.30pm daily) like $1 oysters during the week, this bar and restaurant is an obvious choice for casual dinner, laughs and drinks.

🕐 1100-0200 daily
🏠 1433 Bedford Ave., Crown Heights, 11216 📞 +1 (347) 305 3233
🔗 catfishnyc.com

"It's a neighbourhood bar with great southern food. Try the corn bread!"
– Mike Perry

60 Death & Co.
Map B, P.105

This place mixes the elicit charm of an underground speakeasy with the upscale world of haute cocktail making, and you can expect everything from martinis to punch, as well as a range of aged brown liquors. Marked by a logo-engraved granite doorstep, the cosy boîte runs a strict no-reservation and no-standing policy, and welcomes groups of seven or less. Expect a wait if you go late.

🕐 1800-0200 (Su-Th), -0300 (F-Sa)
🏠 433 E. 6th St., East Village, 10009
☎ +1 (212) 388 0882
URL deathandcompany.com

"Hand-crafted cocktails of the best kind."
– Emmanuel André, TBWA

DISTRICT MAP : **MIDTOWN MANHATTAN (MEATPACKING DISTRICT, CHELSEA, GARMENT DISTRICT)**

- 4_The High Line
- 12_James A. Farley Post Office
- 18_Chelsea Art District
- 25_Chelsea Flea Market
- 44_Pier 66 Maritime Bar & Grill
- 56_Penthouse at Dream
- 58_Le Bain

- 3_FDR Four Freedoms Park
- 9_New York Public Library Main Branch
- 10_Rockefeller Center
- 11_Seagram Building
- 35_Tender Buttons

DISTRICT MAP : **LOWER MANHATTAN (GREENWICH VILLAGE, SOHO, TRIBECA, NOHO)**

- 5_Tribeca Synagogue
- 27_Matter
- 30_Jill Platner
- 37_Caffe Reggio
- 38_Saturdays NYC
- 42_Joe's Pizza
- 49_Fat Cat
- 50_Fanelli Cafe

- 2_Brooklyn Bridge Park
- 41_Buddha Bodai Kosher Vegetarian Restaurant

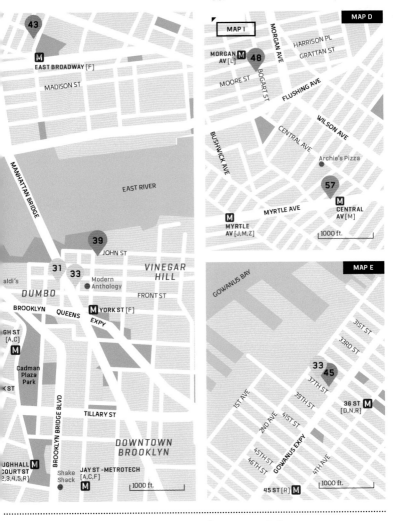

MAP D

MAP I

MAP E

- 7_Jane's Carousel
- 31_Powerhouse @ The Archway
- 33_Brooklyn Flea
- 39_Brooklyn Roasting Company
- 43_Macaron Parlour
- 45_Smorgasburg
- 48_Roberta's
- 57_Bossa Nova Civic Club

DISTRICT MAP : BROOKLYN (COBBLE HILL, CARROLL GARDENS, BOERUM HILL, PROSPECT HEIGHTS)

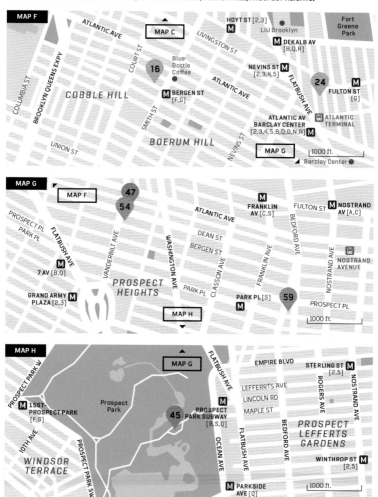

- 16_The Invisible Dog Art Center
- 24_Brooklyn Academy of Music
- 45_Smorgasburg
- 47_Chuko
- 54_Weather Up Brooklyn
- 59_Catfish

MAP I

MAP K

WEST ST

GREENPOINT AV [G] M   GREENPOINT AVE

GREENPOINT AVE

40

WORD

GREEN
POINT

FRANKLIN ST

WEST ST

MESEROLE AVE

36

MANHATTAN AVE.

MCGUINNESS BLVD

EAST RIVER

GEM ST

N 12TH ST

NASSAU AV [G] M

MAP B

KENT AVE

WYTHE AVE

BEDFORD AVE

Mccarren
Park

45

N 8TH ST

46

BERRY ST

Music Hall of
Williamsburg

Blue
Bottle
Coffee

The Meatball
Shop

UNION AVE

BROOKLYN QUEENS EXPY

M

BEDFORD AV [L]

Mast
Brooklyn

Spoonbill &
Sugartown
Books

N 6TH ST

52

KENT AVE

BERRY ST

S 1ST ST

BEDFORD AVE

ROEBLING ST

METROPOLITAN AVE

LORIMER ST [L]
M

29 34

M GRAHAM AVE
[L]

M
METROPOLITAN
AV [G]

LORIMER ST

MANHATTAN AVE

WILLIAMSBURG BRIDGE

S 4TH ST

WILLIAMSBURG

MAP D

1000 ft.

- 29_Desert Island
- 34_Crest Hardware
- 36_Acme Smoked Fish
- 40_Ovenly
- 45_Smorgasburg
- 46_House of Small Wonder
- 52_Maison Premiere

DISTRICT MAP : **UPPER MANHATTAN (CENTRAL PARK, UPPER EAST SIDE), BROOKLYN (ROOSEVELT ISLAND)**

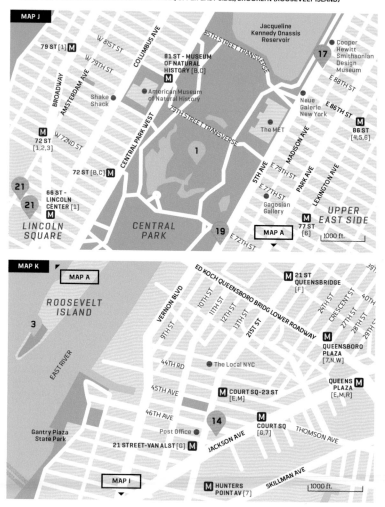

- 1_Central Park
- 3_FDR Four Freedoms Park
- 14_MoMA PS1
- 17_The Guggenheim
- 19_The Frick Collection
- 21_Film Society of Lincoln Center

DISTRICT MAP : **BROOKLYN (ASTORIA), QUEENS (SUNNYSIDE), NEW WINDSOR, NORTHERN MANHATTAN**

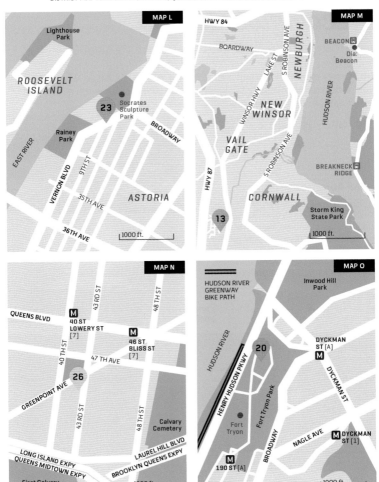

- ● 13_Storm King Art Center
- ● 20_The Met Cloisters
- ● 23_The Noguchi Museum
- ● 26_Johnson Trading Gallery

Accommodation

Hip hostels, fully-equipped apartments & swanky hotels

No journey is perfect without a good night's sleep to recharge. Whether you're backpacking or on a business trip, our picks combine top quality and convenience, whatever your budget.

 < $80 $81–250 $251+

Hôtel Americano

Brought by hotel moguls from Mexico, Hôtel Americano offers 56 ryokan-style rooms, first class amenities and a grill bar next to its roof-top pool in a metal mesh-wrapped boutique lodging next to the High Line. Locally-produced bicycles are available for guests to explore Chelsea and NYC's best galleries around.

🏠 518 W. 27 St., Chelsea, 10001
📞 +1 (212) 216 0000
URL www.hotel-americano.com

The Standard, High Line

Arching over the High Line, The Standard guarantees a taste of urban luxury with top kitchens and a stunning city or Hudson River view from every room. The Top Of The Standard is where Carey Mulligan sang the sad, beautiful *New York, New York* in *Shame* (2011).

🏠 848 Washington St., Meatpacking District, 10014 📞 +1 (212) 645 4646
URL standardhotels.com/high-line

Ace Hotel New York

Lodged into a historic building, Ace displays a shabby-chic style with a 24-hour gym and 275 rooms from small bunk bed chambers to loft suites with an artistic flair. Stumptown Coffee and The Breslin Bar inside Ace are hot tickets for young hipsters in town.

🏠 20 W. 29th St., NoMad, 10001
📞 +1 (212) 679 2222
URL www.acehotel.com/newyork

Paramount Hotel
🏠 235 W. 46th St., Theater District, 10036 📞 +1 (212) 764 5500
URL www.nycparamount.com

Room Mate Grace
🏠 125 W. 45th St., Theater District, 10036 📞 +1 (212) 354 2323
URL room-matehotels.com/en/-grace

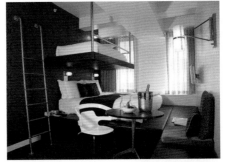

The Jane Hotel

🏠 113 Jane St., Greenwich Village, 10014 📞 +1 (212) 924 6700
URL www.thejanenyc.com

The Local Hostels

🏠 13–02 44th Ave., Long Island City, 11101 📞 +1 (347) 738 5251
URL thelocalny.com

The Bowery Hotel

🏠 335 Bowery, Manhattan, 10003
📞 +1 (212) 505 9100
URL www.theboweryhotel.com

Notes

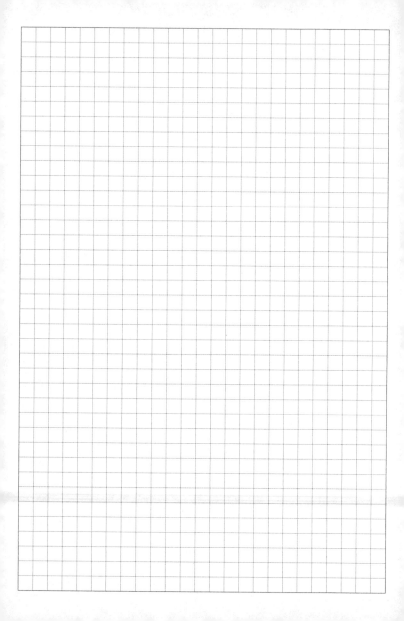

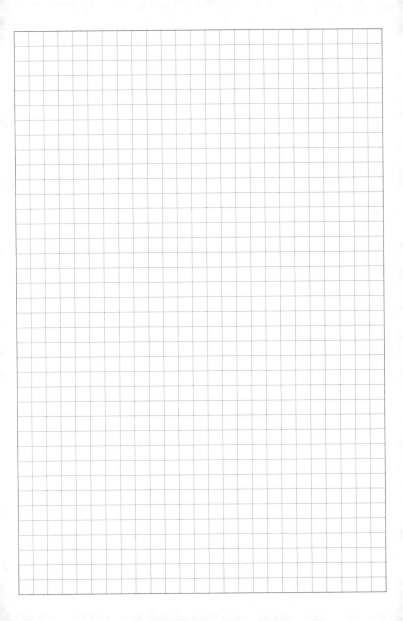

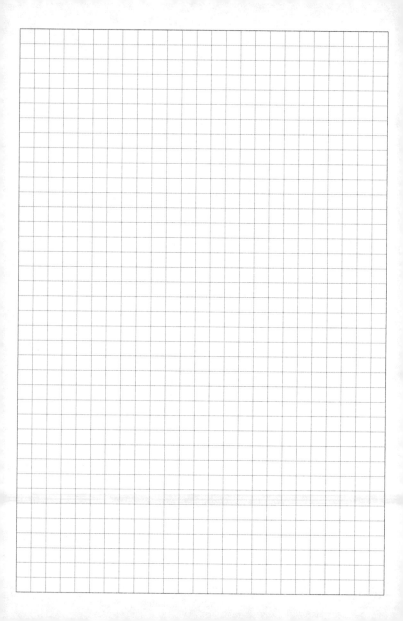

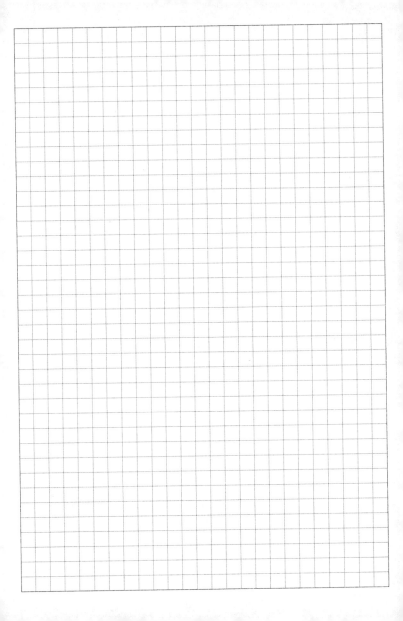

Index

CITIX60

CITIx60: New York

Published and distributed by
viction workshop ltd

viction:ary™

7C Seabright Plaza, 9-23 Shell Street,
North Point, Hong Kong

Url: www.victionary.com
Email: we@victionary.com
🅕 @victionworkshop
🐦 @victionary_
📷 @victionworkshop

Edited and produced by viction:ary

Concept & art direction: Victor Cheung
Research & editorial: Queenie Ho, Caroline Kong
Project coordination: Katherine Wong, Jovan Lip
District map illustration: Yige Wang

Editing: Elle Kwan
Cover map illustration: Mike Perry
Count to 10 illustrations: Guillaume Kashima aka Funny Fun
Photography: Mercedes Noriega

© 2014–2018 viction workshop ltd

All rights reserved. No part of this publication may be reproduced, stored in
retrieval systems or transmitted in any form or by any means, electronic,
mechanical, photocopying, recording or any information storage, without
written permissions of viction:ary.

Content is compiled based on facts available as of April 2018. Travellers are
advised to check out updates from respective locations before your visit.

Seventh edition
ISBN 978-988-78500-2-1
Printed and bound in China

Acknowledgements
A special thank you to all creatives, photographer(s), editors, producers,
companies and organisations for your crucial contributions to our
inspiration and knowledge necessary for the creation of this book. And,
to the many whose names are not credited but have participated in the
completion of the book, we thank you for your input and continuous
support all along.

CITIX60
City Guides

3 1491 01307 5746

CITIx60 is a handpicked list of hot spots that illustrates the spirit of the world's most exhilarating design hubs. From what you see to where you stay, this city guide series leads you to experience the best — the places that only passionate insiders know and go.

Each volume is a unique collaboration with local creatives from selected cities. Known for their accomplishments in fields as varied as advertising, architecture and graphics, fashion, industry and food, music and publishing, these locals are at the cutting edge of what's on and when. Whether it's a one-day stopover or a longer trip, **CITIx60** is your inspirational guide.

Stay tuned for new editions.

City guides available now:

Amsterdam   Portland
Barcelona   Singapore
Berlin   Stockholm
Copenhagen   Taipei
Hong Kong   Tokyo
Istanbul   Vancouver
Lisbon   Vienna
London   San Francisco
Los Angeles
Melbourne
Milan
New York
Paris

NILES - MAINE
DISTRICT LIBRARY

DEC 1 9 2018

NILES, ILLINOIS 60714